Hermetic Lesson 7: The Pleroma

Of The Bad

A. S. Raleigh

Kessinger Publishing's Rare Reprints

Thousands of Scarce and Hard-to-Find Books on These and other Subjects!

- Americana
- Ancient Mysteries
- Animals
- Anthropology
- Architecture
- Arts
- Astrology
- Bibliographies
- Biographies & Memoirs
- Body, Mind & Spirit
- Business & Investing
- Children & Young Adult
- Collectibles
- Comparative Religions
- Crafts & Hobbies
- Earth Sciences
- Education
- Ephemera
- Fiction
- Folklore
- Geography
- Health & Diet
- History
- Hobbies & Leisure
- Humor
- Illustrated Books
- Language & Culture
- Law
- Life Sciences
- Literature
- Medicine & Pharmacy
- Metaphysical
- Music
- Mystery & Crime
- Mythology
- Natural History
- Outdoor & Nature
- Philosophy
- Poetry
- Political Science
- Science
- Psychiatry & Psychology
- Reference
- Religion & Spiritualism
- Rhetoric
- Sacred Books
- Science Fiction
- Science & Technology
- Self-Help
- Social Sciences
- Symbolism
- Theatre & Drama
- Theology
- Travel & Explorations
- War & Military
- Women
- Yoga
- *Plus Much More!*

We kindly invite you to view our catalog list at:
http://www.kessinger.net

LESSON VII.

The Pleroma of the Bad.

2. Now as all these are non-existent in His being, what is there left but Good alone?

For just as naught of bad is to be found in such transcendent Being, so too in no one of the rest will Good be found.

For in them all are all the other things— both in the little and the great, both in each severally and in this living one that's greater than them all and mightiest [of them].

For things subject to birth abound in passions, birth in itself being passible. But where there's passion, nowhere is there Good; and where is Good, nowhere a single passion. For where is day, nowhere is night; and where is night, day is nowhere.

Wherefore in genesis the Good can never *be*, but only be in the ingenerate.

But seeing that the sharing of all things hath been bestowed on matter, so doth it share in Good.

In this way is the Cosmos good, that, in so far as it doth make all things, as far as making goes it's Good, but in all other things it is not Good. For it's both passible and subject unto motion, and maker of things passible.

Now as all these are non-existent in His being, what is there left but Good alone?

All of the things which are of the nature of bad

having been enumerated and all of them having
been seen to be absent from the being of God, it
follows that the sum-total of the bad having been
eliminated from Her, that which remains is of the
nature of the Good; hence, there is in God or Ku
nothing but Good. If so, then She is the Pleroma
of the Good, but if so, the fullness of the Good
being in Her, there can be no part of Good left
for anything else; hence, all Good having been
contained within Her, nothing else but bad will be
left; therefore, all that has been born out from Her
must be bad. The entire realm below Her must,
therefore, be the Pleroma of the Bad as She is
the Pleroma of the Good. If the world without
Her is the Pleroma of the bad, then it contains
the fullness of the bad, and hence, there will not
be left a single bad thing which it does not con-
tain; therefore, there can be no bad thing in Her;
hence, She is absolutely Good.

For just as naught of bad is to be found in
such transcendent Being, so too in no one of
the rest will Good be found.

The very principle of Good can only be found
in Ku. As we have shown, the Good is absolutely
dependent upon those conditions which cannot possibly subsist in anything other than in the Absolute Divine Essence, and were those conditions
which are essential to the very constitution of the
Good present in anything else, they would of
necessity constitute it the Pleroma of the attributes of the Divine Essence, and hence, it would
be the Divine Essence. This would mean that
there were two Absolute Divine Essences; but if
so, there would be no Absolute Divine Essence,
seeing that there can be but one Absolute anything. Thus the Divine Essence itself would be
destroyed. However, we have shown that nothing

can exist, except it be made in the Divine Essence; therefore, this Divine Essence is; hence, nowhere else can Good be found.

For in them all are all the other things—both in the little and the great, both in each severally and in this living one that's greater than them all and mightiest [of them].

In all the Manifestation and the Kosmos below it, are to be found all the things not Good, all the things that are lacking in or absent from Ku. As those things being absent is what constitutes Ku Good, it follows that their presence in the Manifestation and in the Kosmos constitutes it bad, seeing that it is filled with innumerable bad things. This is true both of the greatest and of the smallest parts of it, and of all the intermediary stages between these two extremes. This is true of them all each taken severally and also in the living one, the hylic animal, the Kosmos as a single life or a living creature, in other words, the Kosmos as a whole, as a unit, and also every separate part of it, is bad in all of its attributes. Great and mighty as is the Kosmos, it is essentially bad, because of the fact that the forces that animate it and that cause its diverse transformations are each and all of the nature of bad, and not one of them, partakes of the nature of the Good.

For things subject to birth abound in passions, birth in itself being passible. But where there's passion, nowhere is there Good, and where is Good, nowhere a single passion. For where is day, nowhere is night, and where is night, day is nowhere.

All things that are subject to birth abound in passion, birth in itself being through pas-

sion. All genesis being through passion. All
things generated being generated through passion. For this reason, nothing generated can
possibly be Good, seeing that it is passion
that has generated them. All things that have
been generated through the action of passion,
have embodied the passions that have generated
them and thus partake of those passions. Where
there is passion there can be no such thing as
Good. All bad things are the result of passion.
Passion can never lead to the Good. Passion and
the Good are as far asunder as are the poles as
distinct as the opposition of day and night. Not
one Good thing ever came through passion. In
fact, the Good can never be generated. This is
of course, true seeing that the Good is self-exist
ent; hence, the Good having to be self-existent to
be Good, it cannot be generated by something else,
seeing that if it was, it would lose its character of
self-existence, and hence, would no longer be
Good, but would be bad. Thus because being generated, the fruitage of generation, badness would
inhere in it. In this way it is to be seen that all
things that have come into being through genesis
that is everything that has been generated by
something else, which means the entire Kosmos
and everything that is in it, will be bad per se.

Wherefore, in genesis the Good can never
be, but only be in the ingenerate.

The Good can never be generated, it must at all
times be in that which has never been generated;
hence, in the ingenerate. The Good can never
come into being, seeing that to do so, it will depend upon that which brought it into being and
the very Esse of the Good is to be dependent
upon nothing but itself. God cannot make anything Good, He can only be the Good. As the
Good must be sufficient unto Itself, and needing

nothing from anything except Itself, It can depend upon nothing for anything and still be Good. Thus it is to be seen at once that only the ingenerate, that is that which enjoys endless and beginningless duration within itself and of its own power, can ever be Good. Thus God alone is Good. The Kosmos, both in itself and in each and all of its parts is bad, seeing that it has an engendered existence, and that it came into being, not of itself and through the exercise of its own power, but through the power of God. Being the work of God and not of itself, it is bad. God can do no Good deed, He can only be Good in Himself. The Good can never be engendered.

But seeing that the sharing in all things hath been bestowed on matter, so doth it share in Good.

While God alone is the One in whom Absolute Good is to be found, yet has God constituted matter so that it will mirror and reflect all of His attributes. In this way, is the Goodness of God reflected and mirrored in matter. It has a reflected Good, but not a positive Good as has Ku. Matter has a portion of Good, an element of Good reflected in it, but its true nature is bad and this reflected Good is dominated by the inherent bad. While the Good is but mirrored in matter, the bad is inherently present in it.

In this way is the Cosmos Good; that, in so far as it doth make all things, as far as making goes it's Good, but in all other things it is not Good. For it's both passible and subject unto motion, and maker of things passible.

The Kosmos is Good in so far as it makes all things. It is Good in its capacity as the Maker, but in so far as it is made it is bad. The Kosmos

is made by Ku, and therefore, is it the creature
of genesis, and of passion and in that is it bad.
At the same time, the Kosmos as the living one,
generates the things which it contains, and in this
respect it is Good.   In other words, anything is
Good in what it generates, inasmuch as it has
power over it, but it is bad in so far as it is subject
to generation, and hence, to the power of the one
who generates it.   Inasmuch as it is passible and
subject unto motion, and therefore, the creature
and subject of what is above it, it is bad, but inasmuch as it is capable of making other things passible and subjecting them unto its motions is it
Good.   All situations in which it is the Creator
render it Good, but in all cases where it is created
by Ku, it is bad.   This gives us a perfect criterion
by which we can determine the Good and the bad
that may be in anything.   All things are Good
in so far as they engender something else as their
creatures, but they are bad in so far as they are
engendered by something else.   Therefore, badness consists in being subject to, and dependent
upon something outside itself, while Goodness consists in having something subject to it and dependent upon it for its existence.   To illustrate,
women are Good in so far as they give birth to
children, but they are all bad in so far as they
have been born of woman, and therefore, owe their
life to their having been born.   Goodness then is
nothing other than the measure of one's power,
while badness is nothing other than the measure of
the foreign power to which one may be subject.
The Kosmos then is a mixture of Good and bad;
Good in so far as it is the generator of things, and
bad in so far as it is being generated; Good in so
far as things are subject unto it, but bad in so far
as it is itself subject unto the Will of God and unto
the generative potency of Ku.   On the other hand,

Ku is absolutely Good, because while being generated by nothing and owing Her existence or rather being, to nothing at all, She is the Generatrix and the Maker of all, even the Kosmos itself.

CPSIA information can be obtained
at www.ICGtesting.com
Printed in the USA
LVRC030018101120
671181LV00016BA/77